The Great Ocean Road

A Flash Packers Guide

M Lewis

Copyright © 2014 Author M Lewis

All rights reserved.

ISBN - 10: 1502852004
ISBN-13: 978-1502852007

DEDICATION

FOR ALL OUR FRIENDS THAT HAVE HELPED US ON THE JOURNEY OF LIFE

CONTENTS

1	Introduction	1
2	The Great Ocean Road History	Pg 4
3	Adelaide	Pg 7
4	Adelaide to Portland	Pg 14
5	Portland	Pg 17
6	Port Fairy	Pg 20
7	Warrnambool	Pg 23
8	The Bay of Islands	Pg 26
9	Port Campbell	Pg 31
10	The Twelve Apostles	Pg 34
11	Cape Otway	Pg 39
12	Apollo Bay	Pg 42

THE GREAT OCEAN ROAD

13	Waterfalls and Gullies	Pg 45
14	Lorne	Pg 48
15	Aireys Inlet	Pg 51
16	The Surf Coast	Pg 53
17	Geelong	Pg 56

Split Point Lighthouse

1 INTRODUCTION

An epic journey is the chance for the senses to experience something new. The Great Ocean Road certainly provides the opportunity to experience new sights, to taste new flavours, meet new people, and to discover what may or may not have been discovered before. From the pale sand dunes and teal surf beaches, to the grey rugged cliff faces and clear waterfalls, to the sparse olive heath land and rich green pasture fields, the Great Ocean Road has them all. It cannot be disputed that it is one of the greatest historical scenic touring routes in the world.

We have always enjoyed telling the exciting stories of our travels to our friends and family, hopefully inspiring others to travel a road and to make an iconic journey to build everlasting memories. A friend said to me on our return; "Having followed everyone's holidays this summer, yours is definitely the one I most wanted to be on." Months of planning and dreaming went in to our Great Ocean Road trip. It did not disappoint and it will certainly be one relived for many years after. We have compiled this book of our journey to be used as a travel companion to a journey of the Great Ocean Road, or just enjoyed as travel writing. Unlike most tourists we travelled from West to East, each day driving into a new sun and a new adventure. We travelled in the low season benefitting from cooler weather, cheaper prices and less crowded hotspots. From Adelaide to Melbourne, we have outlined memorable places along the way, and added some useful information for the flash packer, also included are a few areas off the GOR itself but essentially worthy of a visit.

However short or long a journey it can be as adventurous as it is treacherous. Planning, preparation and a backup plan are a must, unless you enjoy living by the seat of your pants. Not just booking accommodation, but researching the best way to see and experience as much as possible to make as much of your time. No one wants to waste their holiday time being sat in a hotel each evening while on the road trying to find accommodation for the next night. Like most flash packers out there, we were on a budget that allowed us to mix good hostels with cheap motels. This book recommends car hire as the best way to take in every sight and smell along the way. This provides the flexibility for stopping as and when the mood takes. However, please take caution when driving the Great Ocean Road as there is nothing more alarming than a car that appears to have been abandoned in the road because the oblivious occupants are out happily taking pictures. The entire tour from beginning to end could take as little as a day or as long as a week. The longer you stay the more you will discover, and why rush something that has so much diversity on offer. Beginning with a little history, and an outline of Adelaide, the journey goes through the main points of interest along the route, flagging up our favourite places. The experiences and memorable moments that we created throughout our journey will hopefully be shared with you.

Dynamite was used to blow away the cliffs to make way for the road

2 THE GREAT OCEAN ROAD HISTORY

Built as a war memorial by returning soldiers from WW1, and named as an Australian National Heritage listed 243km (151 mile) stretch of road, the Great Ocean road runs along the south-eastern coast of the state of Victoria. Officially starting at Torquay, the B100 runs to Warrnambool, linking areas that had previously been difficult to access. The sea and coast are treacherous and infamous for shipwrecks because of hidden rocks and reefs, landings were often delayed or abandoned in bad weather. The overland journeys took coaches months through harsh vegetation. The idea to build a coastal road had been talked about since the 1880's, to link the remote coastal areas and enable timber to be bought up from the Otway areas.

Two business men from Geelong set up the Country Roads Board and the then appointed chairman of the board William Calder proposed the plan for the road. It was backed by the Geelong Mayor Howard Hitchcock, who could see the potential in the road. A budget of 150,000 pounds was set for the hundred miles of road. However, there was plenty of opposition to the plans, as people saw it as a punishment for the returning soldiers and a waste of money, land along the way was subsequently sold off to raise funds. A memorial for Hitchcock can be seen on the road at Mount Defiance near Lorne; unfortunately he died before he could see the road finished.

Originally called; "The South Coast Road" surveying began in 1918. Work started in September 1919 by approximately 3000 returning servicemen of World War One, as a war memorial to those that had given their lives in the Great War. The construction took over 13 years and was done by hand using pick shovel and wheelbarrows. Small machinery and explosives for blasting through the tonnes of rock was also used in the construction. The work was difficult and dangerous in exposed costal mountainous areas and several workers lost their lives while constructing the Great Ocean Road.

After the Great Ocean Road was opened on the 18th March 1922, it has required further work because of storm damage, landslides, bush fires and from an overhanging cliff that collapsed onto the road. All of these events have all caused the road to be closed for months at a time. The first section to be opened from Eastern View to Lorne was then closed in May to December the same year for work and a toll was installed to recoup the construction costs. Tolls of two shillings per motor car or ten shillings for a wagon pulled by more than two horses were taken at Eastern View.

The next section joining Lorne to Apollo Bay took ten years to complete due to the difficult terrain and was opened on Saturday 26th November 1932 by Lieutenant Governor Sir William Irvine. A celebratory ceremony to give the road the title of the world's longest war memorial was held at the Lorne Grand Pacific Hotel. The tolls were removed by October 1936 and the road deeds were officially handed to the Victorian State Government.

In 1962 the Tourist Development Authority named it; "...one of the world's great scenic roads", in 2011 it was added to the Australian National Heritage List. Finally in 2004 the 'Great Ocean Walk' was opened which included 104km of walking trails that follow the coastline.

Kookaburra and many other birds can be found in Australia.

3 ADELAIDE

Adelaide the capital city of the state of South Australia nestles beautifully between the Mount Lofty range and the sea. Designed by Colonel William Light, in a grid layout known as Light's Vision, the city square mile is bordered by the four terraces; north, south east and west. Victoria Square marks the centre, and each of the quadrants has a park at their centre. King William Street runs north to south, and all the streets are named after prominent settlers, Commissioners appointed by the British Government, and directors of the South Australian Company. Some of these never visited or lived in South Australia, but were influential in setting up the colony and overseeing the establishment of some of the laws that defined it. Heading north of the city you will cross the River Torrens into North Adelaide to find the Oval Stadium. To the east, the suburbs of Norwood and Kensington stretch towards the Mount Lofty range. Heading in a south west direction will take you through an industrial area to the popular beach of Glenelg, and the airport sits conveniently to the west of the city.

Adelaide has done well to preserve some of its most iconic buildings of historical interest as the city has developed. The old is mixed in with the new and there is something for every generation. A range of shopping centres for every budget, the central market with its delicious range of food and drink and a visit to the quaint village of Hahndorf, there is plenty to keep the flash packer busy while still keeping hold of the purse strings.

Memorable Moments;

Hahndorf;

Hahndorf is Australia's oldest German settlement, and is twenty minutes from the city, direct buses run regularly to the main street; weekends see them left with standing room only packed out with locals and tourists alike. Sundays the bus service is reduced, return from the opposite side of the street, or travel on to the town of Mount Barker. There are a multitude of shops, eateries in which to try a schnitzel and a few pubs along the main street.

Adelaide Botanic Gardens;

The entrance gates sit on the junction of east and north terrace, the Botanic gardens has an extensive collective stretched over its 125 acres. Visit the impressive tropical palm house, see a double coconut in the museum of botany with its collection boasting as being one of the largest in the southern hemisphere, have a look at Flinders journal and map, or take a peek at the giant water lilies in the humid Amazon pavilion. Free entry and guided walks, its open daily during daylight hours.

Adelaide Gaol

Just off the tram line from north terrace, the gaol has seen over 300,000 inmates housed in its 147 years of operation before it closed in 1988, making it the longest continuously operating prison in Australia. Tours are self guided so you can spend as long as you like in the eerie west tower where executions took place and the smell of death still lingers, between the inner and outer walls of the gaol are the graves of those executed, including the only woman to be executed in South Australia, and was later found to be wrongly convicted. Well worth a visit, open every day except Saturdays, and check the website to book an evening ghost tour. (www.adelaidegoal.sa.gov.au)

Central Market

Adelaide central market can be accessed from Victoria Square, or jump off the free bus that stops outside, open Tuesday to Saturday and late night Friday. More than just a market, with over eighty stalls trading in; delicious cheese, olives, rich coffee, tasty yoghurt and many other fine foods homemade dishes and fresh produce, a must for food lovers, sit and eat in or buy for later. (www.adelaidecentralmarket.com.au)

SA Museum

Situated on north terrace the museum is open daily and free to get in except for the special exhibitions. The ground floor hosts a nice cafe, shop and a host of mammals from around the world, take the time to visit the upper floors and see the impressive minerals, fossils and biodiversity collections. Learn about different boomerang shapes and how they are made in the Aboriginal culture section. (www.samuseum.sa.gov.au)

Cleland Conservation Park

Jump on a bus up to Crafers Ramp, and change on to the bus for Cleland Conservation Park, check bus times or you may miss one of the only three buses a day. Entrance fee is a little pricey, but worth it for the view back over the city. Walk among the animals that you may miss the opportunity to see otherwise; the endangered dingoes, wombats and Tasmanian devils. For an extra fee get close enough to a koala to smell his eucalyptus breath and even have your picture taken holding these lovely furry fellows, bred in captivity and awake for only an hour a day, the keepers are careful to ensure they don't stay awake too long. Check their website for special events and night walks; it does not have the enclosed feel of a park as you follow the trail through the kangaroo and emu enclosures, with possum jumping across your path.

Mount Lofty

On the same road to Cleland Park is Mount Lofty Summit, experience the best views of Adelaide from here some 700 metres above sea level. Visit the information centre, sit in the restaurant or have a wander around the surrounding tracks.

(www.mtloftysummit.com)

Wine Museum

With over 38,000 bottles of wine, chosen from all over the states of Australia, the ambient atmosphere created inside makes it a perfect place to learn about and try whatever flavour takes your fancy. Have a wander around and find out how and why wines taste different, see the impressive cork and wine label collection. Every other Friday the Uncorked events provide music and speciality wines by the glass make an evening of your visit and order from their menu. (www.wineaustralia.com.au)

Useful Information;

From when you land at the airport or train station, Adelaide has an efficient and regular bus service that runs to and from the suburbs and around the city centre, into the night. A metro card can be purchased at the airport bus stop, or at the Metro centre on King William street, and as long as you have credit enjoy cheaper travel than paying for individual journeys. There are a network of free buses around the city centre that loop in both directions, taking a route around North Adelaide and past the zoo, train station, market and Oval. Taxis are metered and not cheap; a surcharge is added from the airport. Domestic and international arrivals are all at the one terminal, a taxi rank can be found just outside. The tram line runs all the way from the entertainment centre to Glenelg beach, with a free stretch inside the city. The Metro card can be used on buses and trams. Situated just off the high street down James Place, the Tourist

Information office and its helpful friendly locals, have a plethora of local knowledge, guides and maps. Bus and tram timetables can be picked up from the Metro centre, or downloaded at; www.adelaidemetro.com.au .

Around the city centre there are plenty of back packer hostels to choose from, even the cheapest hotel around this area the main area is pricey. If you are staying for more than a few days it is worth looking into an apartment, there are plenty to choose from with residents converting back rooms for rental. Check out the websites; www.airbnb.com www.stayz.com.au or www.homeaway.com.au . Save money on accommodation without a breakfast, and make use of their fridge and cooking facilities.

Between North Terrace and Grenfell Street are the main shopping centres, the Myer Centre, City Cross and Rundle Mall complete with food courts' providing a wide variety of cuisine; burritos, fresh sandwiches, and jacket potatoes. Southern Cross Arcade has an extensive affordable and quality range of Asian food, or look towards the Central Market for a taste of something homemade, the Ace's bar in the centre of the market has a pizza oven and a lunchtime specials board. Look out for the specials on pub lunches; The London situated between North Terrace and the Myer centre does a succulent steak pie with mash, while the Mansions near the north end of Pulteney Street offers a good value steak and chips lunch.

THE GREAT OCEAN ROAD

The Southern Ocean

4 ADELAIDE TO PORTLAND

Adelaide to Portland is a fairly direct journey that will take around a day, passing south of the small town of Murray Bridge and skirting around Mount Gambier, pasture land and vineyards eventually give way to timber forests. Leaving Adelaide the National Highway steeply travels up the Mount Lofty range, through a tunnel along the hill tops and seems to never fall away. Look out for kangaroos in the fields and koala in the trees. The Swanport Bridge is built three miles south of the town of Murray Bridge and the original bridge; which was the first built to cross the murky waters of the River Murray. River life such as platypus, Murray cod, trout, perch, Murray crayfish, and the short necked Murray turtle can be found. The River Murray also provides water back to Adelaide. The road runs parallel to a railway track, making a right turn just before the town of Keith. Keith has a population of no more than a thousand, a farming town of sheep and lucernes, with the attraction of a land rover on a pole, a small detour for those interested. Continuing on the highway the opportunities of stopping at a restroom are few and far between. Pasture land gives way to vineyard and after vineyard, as the A8 turns into the A66 at the town of Keith there is a restroom and car park area. The Riddoch Highway is quite a basic road; climbing up to the speed limit endangers drivers of hitting one of the many potholes in the roads poor surface. Cutting through the Padthaway National Park, and acres of the South Australian blue gum trees, manna gum and stringy bark trees, the highway comes to the town of Naracoote. Naracoote Caves National Park; South Australia's only World Heritage site has a network of over twenty caves. The caves stay at a constant 17 degrees centigrade and contain fossil deposits from mega fauna that became extinct over 60,000 years ago, when the Southern ocean used to be 100 kilometres further inland than it is today. Continuing on through the Glen Roy and Penola Conservation Park the road heads east onto the A1. The Princes Highway begins just before the town of Mount Gambier, and continues on through the protected snow gum trees of the Myora Forest Reserve. Mount Gambier is famous for its blue lake that sits in a crater and is said to change its colour every year. It is well worth an overnight stop to fully appreciate the beauty of the area and visit the highest point at the historic Centenary Tower. Crossing unknowingly over into the state of Victoria, and crossing an international time line the clocks are forwards of South Australia by half an hour. The Cobboboonee National Park in Victoria, recognises the Aboriginal traditional land owners, but has been an area much disputed over as the government sells the rights to chipping companies in fragmented parcels, infuriating local people and stranding wildlife.

Portland is signposted from the A1, follow the A200 into Portland and an information centre can be found by following the blue and yellow "i" signs to the foreshore.

One of the many old buildings in Portland.

5 PORTLAND

Portland is the oldest European settlement in the state of Victoria; it provided shelter from the rough weather of the Bass Straits for the whalers and sealers. It is the only deep sea port between Adelaide and Melbourne therefore an important feature on the coastline. The Portland Wind Energy Project sees the area with the biggest wind farm in the Southern Hemisphere, the giant turbines making an unmistakable mark on the landscape. Portland still has evidence of its important past as a trading port. Fishing and wool have now given way to; aluminium, and huge grain, woodchip and sand loaders take a prominent position in the back ground of Henty Bay. Take a walk around the towns' historical buildings, with over two hundred remaining it is difficult not to glimpse one of the well preserved buildings from the 1800's. The 1849 Customs House which is still used for the same purpose, the old Post Office, the impressive St.Macs Hotel with its third storey balcony, and many more can be taken in on a self guided historical buildings walk, pick up a guide from the tourist information centre that sits on the foreshore.

Memorable Moments;

A short drive from Portland will take you to Cape Bridgewater and there begins the incredible coastal sights of this journey. Bridgewater Bay and its white sandy beaches stretch back towards the dunes beyond. A cafe and restroom are situated by the beach car park. Drive on further up the hill and here begins the long coastal walk to the seal lookout, observe the signs and be prepared for a three hour walk to glimpse the colony of fur seals. The road continues to the Petrified Forest and blowhole look out; take care to stay to the tracks to help preserve the delicate structures. From the viewpoint you get a real sense of the power of the Southern Ocean as it crashes and sprays up metres above the pillowed lava rocks below. Its captivating watching the foamy waters running back down through the rocks forming channels and gullies, you may be lucky enough to spot a Southern right whale here in winter and spring. Once a volcanic island, erosion by millions of years of rainfall have hardened into stunning natural formations. The Petrified Forest is a truly awesome site on a grand scale, acres of piped shape tubules stretch out across the landscape, and one can imagine a forest having once been there. Named the Petrified Forest because it was thought sand covered a forest, petrifying it for all time, but actually formed by sand and water dissolving the limestone, cementing into trunk shapes as the water seeps down.

Useful Information;

Although only a small town, Portland is an ideal location to

explore the coastline; the Petrified Forest and blowholes are a truly spectacular detour. Staying overnight here enables one to start the first leg of the GOR journey fresh and relaxed. Portland information centre can be found by following the blue and yellow "i" signs to the foreshore, along this same road are a choice of fish and chip shops, selling today's freshest catch. For friendly budget accommodation; head out of town towards the lighthouse, situated as close to the cliff tops as you can get is; Bellevue back packers on Sheoke Road, units have TV fridge and cooking facilities, clean linen is provided.
(www.visitportland.com.au)

Cape Bridgewater – The Petrified Forest

6 PORT FAIRY

Leaving Portland, follow the A1 Princes Highway to Port Fairy; where the Moyne River joins the Southern Ocean. This coastal town was the site of an old whaling station, although any scrap of evidence of its history has been eradicated, except being named after a whaling ship that sheltered here from a storm. One of the busiest ports in Australia during the 1800's, wool, wheat and gold were loaded to ships in the bay bound for England. Moyne Mill; a five storey bluestone flour mill remains in the main wharf area.

Memorable Moments;

Griffiths Island can be walked around in just over an hour. On the eastern tip of the island stands the solar and wind powered lighthouse, made of local bluestone in 1859, the spiral slab steps inside are built into the outside wall. Follow the circular track around the back of the island and you may spot; the protected mutton birds, small brown wallaby and kangaroo. Beware of snakes hiding out in the long grasses, the track is at times uneven and crosses the beach.

Tower Hill Reserve is off the highway fifteen minutes east of Port Fairy; follow the one way track that winds down through the craters to the large car park area, toilets and conic shaped visitor centre. It's hard to believe this area was cleared by European settlers for farming, and then left barren before being restored and replanted by local people to what it is today. Victoria's first National Park, Tower Hill sits inside an extinct volcano formed some 60,000 years ago. Lookout for a variety of wildlife including; emu, koala, and kangaroo; are amongst the abundance of birds and animals that roam here. A variety of tracks levelled in difficulty are signposted around the rim of the crater, through the forest and across the wetlands via a boardwalk. On leaving on the one way track, make a left turn up the hill to the lookout for the best views across the park and another chance to spot kangaroo or emu before returning to the main road.

Useful Information;

Pick up Regent Street or Bank Street off the A1 towards the Moyne River, following it south for Griffiths Island; there are a few car parks as Ocean Drive meets Gipps Street. The main centre is awash with eateries and cafes, or enjoy some locally produced confectionary, a tourist information centre can be found on Bank Street. (www.portfairy.com.au)

Port Fairy Griffiths Island

7 WARRNAMBOOL

Warrnambool named by the indigenous people for its close proximity to a volcano, marks the start of the GOR. Sitting on the 130km stretch of shipwreck coast between Port Fairy to Cape Otway, the coast has seen over 600 ships run aground, around 60 of them outside Lady Bay. A fairly inconsequential town, yet the largest on the GOR, Warrnambool never really developed itself as an major port, due to the landing difficulties caused by the bay. One of the main reasons to add this town to your itinerary would be to spot a whale, or attend one its annual festivals. On the east of the city Logan's Beach is a recognised nursery area for the Southern Right whales, sightings have grown in number since whaling was outlawed back in 1935. The purpose built viewing platform makes it one of the most easily accessible and advantageous places to spot a whale along this stretch of coastline. The town has a few historic buildings remaining; an 1870's built post office and courthouse.

Memorable Moments;

Logan's beach whale viewing platform sees the arrival of female whales from May to August. Seeking warmer waters, the males and young adults remain further out to sea, while the females give birth and rear the whale calf close to the shore. Logan's beach is easy to find, just follow the signs from the town, crossing over Hopkins River to Hopkins Point Road, the zigzagged structure of the platform gives good shelter from the elements.

Allansford is a small town that marks the join between Princes Highway and the start of the GOR. As you make the right turn onto the B100, a short distance down the road Cheese World Museum shop and cafe appears on the left. The factory itself stands on the opposite side of the road, a fairly new build as unfortunately fire had destroyed the two previous factories that stood in the same spot. The shop is well worth a stop to stock up on local produce, try a milkshake or use the amenities.

Useful Information;

The town has a good range of amenities, accommodation, shops and nice restaurants making it ideal for an overnight stay. There is a good choice of motels in the town, check out; the Cally Hotel (www.callyhotel.com.au) on Fairy Street, double and single rooms above a friendly pub that also has a good menu, Wi-Fi and a large car park at the rear. Bojangles (www.bojanglespizza.com) on Liebig Street serves tasty pasta and pizza to dine in or take out. Across the street is a tasty looking Mexican restaurant or fish and chip shop. A visitor centre can be found on Merri Street. Around Lady Bay there are plenty of sandy beaches ideal for swimming, behind this is a large adventure park. North east of the city is the picturesque Hopkins Falls. The main reason to linger would have to be the chance of seeing a whale close to the shore in Logan's Bay. Following the road east out of Warrnambool on the Princes Highway, a right turn will take you onto the B100 and the start of the GOR. (www.visitwarrnambool.com.au)

The Bay of Islands Coastal Park

8 THE BAY OF ISLANDS

From Warrnambool the landscape begins to change, as the GOR winds towards Peterborough and Port Campbell. From pastureland to heath lands, the road winds along the cliff tops, there are many sign posted points of interest. The Bay of Islands Coastal Park stretches 32km to meet Port Campbell National Park. View the spectacular ocean in all its ferocity and the rock stacks it has carved from several lookouts. Look for wildlife that has cleverly taken refuge and formed colonies on the rock stacks out at sea, safe from the predators of the main land, such as; rare Black-faced Cormorants, silver gulls, Australasian Gannets, Wandering Albatross and Mutton birds. Look down to see little penguins that have made their homes on the beaches below.

During the summer always be bush fire ready, be aware of changing conditions. During winter be aware of weather causing subsidence of the cliffs; always stick to the marked paths. Follow the marked tracks from the designated parking areas;

they are all varying distances from the car parks.

Boat Bay – this narrow beach has deep calm waters thanks to the offshore reef. A steep ramp is used for boat launching.

Bay of Islands – this viewpoint is worth a stop as a beginning of the appreciation of the limestone stacks that have been carved by the Southern ocean.

Bay of Martyrs – from this platform look back across Massacre Bay, named after the horrid incident in the 1800's, where a group of local aboriginals were herded off the cliffs to their deaths below by European settlers.

Halladale Point – named after the "Falls of Halladale" a ship wrecked in 1908, accessible by following the track from the southern end of the car park for the Bay of Martyrs, the track continues on to Wild Dog Cove.

Wild Dog Cove – explore rock pools and enjoy the shallow paddling of this beach, access is from Peterborough, near the golf course.

The Grotto – follow the steps down to get close up to the ocean in all its wonder as it meets the cliffs. Well worth the trek down the steps to a natural open cave below and marvel at the coloured pools of water.

London Bridge – has an upper and lower viewing platform. It was once possible to walk across London Bridge, erosion formed two natural archways. Until 1990 when a partial collapse left tourists stranded on the outer part, they were rescued unharmed by helicopter. Now it is sometimes referred to as London Arch.

The Arch –different to the London Arch, from the viewing platform the water can be seen gushing through the rock causing a waterfall affect and eroding and carving the archway. Has a similar look to the Durdle Door in Dorset UK.

Two Mile Bay – a long path links this point to the town scenic lookout. There is a track to the beach, but rocks and reefs make it a hazardous area.

Town Scenic Lookout – looks out over the town of Port Campbell providing a great view of the natural harbour. The lookout can be accessed from the car park or a walk up from Port Campbell Bay; the steps are at the end of the beach.

Maps of the area and the coastal walks along with up to date

THE GREAT OCEAN ROAD

park information can be found for all Victoria parks at;
www.parkweb.vic.gov.au .

The Grotto

The Arch

9 PORT CAMPBELL

The town of Port Campbell is an ideal port of call on the GOR, nestled in the Port Campbell National Park. Only a short drive from the Bay of Islands and fifteen minutes north of the Twelve Apostles makes it an ideal place to make an overnight stop. Tourism and fishing supports this small town with a population of around 600. Port Campbell was named in the 1800's by Captain Alexander Campbell a whaler that frequently sailed the Bass Straits and sought shelter in the bay.

Memorable Moments;

A good view of the town can be appreciated from the lookout situated on the cliff tops at the far end of the beach. The beach is sandy and is an interesting place to see what has been washed up amongst the seaweed, follow the beach along and walk up Campbell Creek. Have a walk along the jetty, and see the remains of the old pier. Here once stood a rocket launcher; used to winch in survivors of shipwrecks, the success depended upon the accuracy of the rocket launcher.

Useful Information;

Turning off the GOR in to the main street of Port Campbell; Lord Street will take you down to the beach front. Lord Street has a couple of pubs, Nico's pasta and pizza, and a convenience store. On the corner of Cairns Street is a very cosy pub overlooking the beach; 12 Rocks Cafe Beach bar (www.12rocksbeachbar.com.au), serving hearty meals and homemade cakes. Across the road are a fish and chip shop and ample car parking. Port Campbell has a range of accommodation; the Holiday Park on Morris Street overlooks the Port Campbell Creek, on the main street choose from villas or a Motel. The best value is the new build, highly rated back packers hostel (www.portcampbellhostel.com.au)on Tregea Street; clean and well equipped with off road parking, the communal areas are large open plan free Wi-Fi zones, bikes can also be hired from here. The Port Campbell visitor information centre situated on Morris Street is open daily and has a great display of shipwreck artefacts, some salvaged from the Loch Ard. Pick up maps of the area, coastal walks and information on the Twelve Apostles or buy one of the lovely souvenirs.

(www.visit12apostles.com.au)

THE GREAT OCEAN ROAD

Port Campbell Bay

10 THE TWELVE APOSTLES

Heading out of Port Campbell along the GOR through the Twelve Apostles Marine National Park there are a few more points of interest for historians and wildlife enthusiasts.

Memorable Moments;

Mutton bird Island is a nesting site for the protected Mutton birds or the Short-tailed Shearwater as they are sometimes known. Once hunted as a good source of food, the birds arrive around September time after a 30,000km trip. Building their nests they are most active around January and February until they migrate again in April. The Loch Ard sailing ship sank in 1878 on the corner of Mutton bird Island. The Loch Ard was sailing to Melbourne from England, a heavy cargo ship with crew and passengers it hit a reef in heavy fog. The ship broke up before the lifeboats could be launched and sank within minutes. Of the 54 crew and passengers on board only two survived.

Clinging to wreckage for hours Tom Pearce was washed into the bay at Loch Ard Gorge he heard Eva Carmichael shouting and he went back in and rescued her. He climbed out of the gorge and went for help; unfortunately it was too late for the rest of the passengers. A large porcelain peacock was amongst the luxury goods in the cargo, some were washed up in the Gorge, some later salvaged by dive teams. Along with other items from the ship it can be seen on display at the Flagstaff Hill Maritime Museum in Warrnambool. Mutton bird Island viewing platform has an upper and lower view and is only a short distance from the car park.

Loch Ard Gorge is the next stop off along the road, and there is plenty to see and explore here. There are three different lengthy self guided walks around the cliff tops with information points along the way. From the main car park the path to the lookout looks out of the gorge really give a feel of how treacherous the sea can be. Stairs from the lookout take you down to the beach to explore the inlet where Tom was washed ashore, at the rear of the beach are some impressive rock formations making it worth the trek down. Follow the circular symbols for the geology walk, this takes in more views of the coastline and Island Archway. The triangular symbols take a walk following the story of the shipwreck and to the cemetery. On beyond this take the living on the edge walk and follow the square symbols, this takes in the lookout at Broken Head and Thunder Cave. This special area is worthy of note as its importance in history and some interesting geological features, allow two to three hours to take it all in.

The Twelve Apostles Visitor Centre is the next stop en route and is the jewel in the crown, if you have been amazed at this coastlines beauty before, then be prepared to be amazed again. Parking in the designated areas, a road under pass has been built allowing tourists to get to the viewing platforms safely. At the far end of the car park is also the take off point for helicopter rides. The visitor centre has a refreshment area, sells souvenirs and local produce. Following the walkway in either direction will provide many angles to get a good photograph of this iconic location. Originally named the "Sow and Piglets", later the "Apostles" and then the "Twelve Apostles" there are now eight stacks remaining intact. Due to weather and erosion over millions of years the stacks formed firstly as cracks and caves, and over time large parts have broken away. Although only eight apostles stand the landscape is ever changing, and new stacks are expected as the waves continue to erode the headland. Hundreds of thousands of tourists arrive in the area every year to get a snap of Victoria's coastline, try to time your visit to avoid the bustle.

Gibson Steps are a short drive from the visitor centre; a small car park is signposted on the cliff top side of the road. There is a lookout with a glimpse of two corner stacks, or take the 86 steep steps down to the beach. Although thought to have carved out by aboriginals, they are named after Hugh Gibson; a European settler in the area. The beach can be walked along in either direction, beware of weather and tides if you venture towards the headlands. The steps and beach can be particularly hazardous in high tides as the waves will come right up to the cliffs; popular with fishermen it is not suitable for swimming.

THE GREAT OCEAN ROAD

The Twelve Apostles Marine National Park has many incredible limestone stacks.

Loch Ard Gorge

11 CAPE OTWAY

Cape Otway sits on the southern tip of the Otways, made up of the Great Otway National Park and the Otways Forest Park. The GOR takes an inland turn from Princetown as it heads through the forests of the Great Otway National Park. The road winds upwards almost as to be driving in the tree tops. It was declared a park in 2004 when several smaller parks and reserves amalgamated and now covers over 100,000 hectares. The park is so large and diverse it has beaches, steep cliffs, gullies waterfalls, and tall forests. The Otway Forest Park has been logged for timber for more than 150 years. Koala, kangaroo, wallabies, kookaburras and many other species can be found in their natural habitat here. Cape Otway got its name back in 1800, when one of the first European ships sailed through and named it after the Captain Albany Otway. The lighthouse was built in 1848 and used all the way through until 2004, making it the longest continuous operating light on the mainland.

Memorable Moments;

Cape Otway Road leaves the GOR and heads towards the cape and lighthouse. This road is worth veering off the track, as koala can be spotted in the trees. Look to the areas of dead manna gum trees that they have already stripped bare. The chance of a sighting of a koala awake and eating is high as the area is highly populated with these sleepy furry creatures. Look for slow movements in the higher branches as they only ever come to ground briefly to change trees, sleeping in the nooks of the branches and trunk for around 20 hours a day. They are very select over the Eucalyptus leaves they eat, carefully sniffing and selecting before eating. They will consume around a kilogram of leaves a day, quite a large amount for such a small animal. There are lay-bys along the road, take care to pull in off this busy winding track.

Cape Otway lighthouse is the oldest officially built lighthouse on the mainland. It is a long way down the road to the precinct area within which the lighthouse is now enclosed. A high fee is charged to access the precinct including; the lighthouse, radar room and telegraph station, and the cafe situated in the old lighthouse keepers cottage. There are toilet facilities and a short circular walking route beyond the car park, but it provides no real views of either lighthouse or coast. The best views are from the 90 metre tall light house, you may spot whales and dolphins in the Bass Straits. (www.lightstation.com)

Useful Information;

The GOR walk continues to follow the coastline through the park and up to Apollo Bay. There are many camp sites, picnic areas and visitor areas dotted around the park with varying facilities. Johanna Beach has a large area for tents and caravans, Aire River is smaller and shady, and Blanket Bay is in a nice spot near the beach. (An entire list can be found at www.coastalcampingvictoria.com.au).There is bed and breakfast available at the light house keepers' cottage. There are a number of activities available in the park including; horse riding, tree top walks and mountain biking. Fuel stations are few en route; Apollo Bay and Lavers Hill are the nearest main towns with services.

Koala can be found in abundance in Cape Otway

12 APOLLO BAY

The GOR returns to the coast line at the beach town of Apollo Bay, still within the vast body of the Great Otway National Park. After much driving under the canopy of the Otways Forest, Apollo Bay is situated at the bottom of the slopes. A pristine horse shoe shaped beach stretches into the sea, with the Otway ranges framing the picture. Apollo Bay is the perfect place to relax and take stock of the many incredible sights on the journey so far. A small and quiet town with a population of around 1000, it has been popular in the past with; timber cutters, fishermen and whalers. The whaling station was at Point Bunbury, where the golf course is now. The bay was named in 1845 when the Apollo ship sheltered here from a storm. Its importance as a town increased after 1932 when the GOR was completed making it more accessible. Apollo Bay is now popular with tourists visiting the Otways, and its sheltered position makes it popular for; swimming, fishing, diving, swimming and boating activities.

Memorable Moments;

The Museum is situated in the old Cable Station; a small building on the way out of the town built in 1936. From this point an undersea cable provided the first connection between Tasmania and the mainland. A photographic history of the area, and some salvage from shipwrecks is on display.

Useful Information;

The GOR runs along the foreshore and is lined with a variety of clothes and surf shops. There are a good variety of restaurants including; Italian, Thai and Chinese and a food court offering value seafood freshly cooked and good oven baked pizza. Out of season some of the shops are closed for winter. Supermarkets and convenience stores have shorter winter opening hours but stock all the basics. On Saturday there is a community market. There is a range of accommodation available in the town from; chalets and houses on long term lets, to cheaper motels and backpackers. Surfside Backpackers (www.surfsidebackpacker.com) offers comfortable double and single room as well as dormitories at reasonable rates. Suitable for the flash packer, the views from the garden and lounge area are superb, with separate bathrooms, a choice of kitchens, pool room and TV lounge. The information centre in Apollo Bay is situated right on the foreshore.

The Otways National Park

13 WATERFALLS AND GULLIES

Along the GOR water has carved a path to the sea, leaving beautiful gullies and waterfalls through the rocks and land. On the stretch of road between Apollo Bay and Lorne this beauty is on display minutes from the road. Numerous opportunities to stop and admire these creeks, the rock formations and crystal clear water would add days on your journey. Sheoak Falls and Grey River are two that stand out.

Grey River road is a small turning off the GOR in the small township of Grey River. Look for a car park and on the left of this Grey River road heads between some residential units and up into the park, soon becoming a gravel track. Koalas can be sighted in the nooks and branches of many of the trees as you head along the road as they are abundant in this area. It is becoming a popular tourist stopping place, and is attracting wildlife such as lorikeets to the picnic area.

Sheoak Falls is a sign posted picnic area shortly before the town of Lorne. There are two signposted walks from the car park, as shown on the information board. The circular route is a challenging climb of around two hours and also includes Swallow Cave. For the shorter route to the falls follow the path that leads to the right of the car park entrance. The path climbs and then flattens out and provides a good look out over the GOR. The path dips down and follows the gully to the waterfall; it is quite well hidden and cannot be heard until you are closer too. Beware the path can be muddy and slippy after rains. About 15 metres high, the crystal clear water crashes down over the dark rock faces into a deep pool below. Sheoak Falls is one of the few places where such a spectacular waterfall of such magnitude can be seen so close to the road. Return to the car park along the same track to avoid the longer route.

THE GREAT OCEAN ROAD

Sheoak Falls

14 LORNE

The beautiful seaside town of Lorne on Louttit Bay began to develop as a tourist destination after the GOR was extended in 1922. The Grand Pacific Hotel was the site of the celebrations in 1932 that marked the long awaited opening of the road between Lorne and Apollo Bay. The bay is named after a Captain who was retrieving cargo from a shipwreck nearby and sought shelter from a storm in the bay. The early European settlers in the area were timber cutters. Rudyard Kipling visited the area and wrote a poem that included references to Lorne and the Erskine River.

Memorable moments;

Take some time to get up to Teddy's Lookout on George Street to get some good views of the town and the coastline. Erskine Falls are some 8km out of the town within the Great Otway National Park, another beautiful natural waterfall in this picturesque area. Wander down the new or old pier, the old tram tracks can still be seen that were used to transport the timber to waiting ships until the 1930's. Have a chat with the fishermen, the locals are always happy to share a tale of what creatures of the deep have been spotted in the area.

Mount Defiance Lookout is a few kilometres before Lorne and provides good views up and down the coast line; beware when pulling into the small car park as it is on the coast side of the road on a sharp bend.

Eastern View Memorial Arch is what you would expect to start or finish the GOR, but actually sits between Lorne and Aireys Inlet. There is a bronze sculpture depicting returned soldiers and information signs. This is the fourth attempt at a memorial arch, the first was removed, the second destroyed by a truck, and the third archway was destroyed in the Ash Wednesday fires of 1983. It is a popular photo stop; there is a car park after the archway, please park off the road carefully and considerately.

Useful Information

There are a range of shops in the town along the foreshore road including; craft and books shops, a supermarket and a range of fresh locally made produce. The main place to hang around is the pier. Here you will find the restaurants with the best views and catch of the day, albeit a little expensive. There is ample car parking around the pier and toilet facilities. Accommodation in the area is limited to high range hotels or camping. (www.lovelorne.com.au)

Eastern View Memorial Arch o the road between Lorne and Aireys Inlet

15 AIREYS INLET

Aireys Inlet is a small town popular with surfers and has been used for several filming settings. Named in 1842 after a settler by the name of John Airey the area is famous for its Split Point Lighthouse. The 34 metre tall lighthouse, originally called Eagles Nest Point, was built in 1891 with 132 stairs; the lantern room is now also used as a mobile phone base station. The Lighthouse overlooks an Inlet and the horse shoe shaped Step Beach.

Memorable Moments;

Take a walk up and around the Split Point Lighthouse, 30 minute tours now take visitors up inside the balcony room. Follow Lighthouse Road to the car park at the top, there is then a short walk to the Lighthouse. Walk along the track behind the Lighthouse to look out over Eagle Rock. A circular walk heads downhill to Painkalac Creek; past a playground, toilets and a picnic area, a replica bark hut and continues through the wetland area before heading uphill towards the car park. (www.splitpointlighthouse.com.au)

Useful Information;

Just off the main road is a General Store. A cute Teahouse is situated a short walk on the road to the Lighthouse, selling tasty homemade treats and souvenirs. Surf and strong currents in this area can be dangerous, swimmers and surfers need to beware of the strong rip tides. (www.aireysinlet.org.au)

Wetland area at Painkalac Creek Aireys Inlet

16 THE SURF COAST

From Aireys Inlet to Torquay the coastline is known for its fantastic surf beaches. The main hub of shops and spots for the best surf are situated around Torquay, and it is the official start of the GOR. Bells Beach between Torquay and Anglesea is most famous for hosting the Rip Curl Pro Surfing competition around Easter time. Anglesea was originally known as Swampy Creek and has a large population of western grey kangaroos around the golf course. The main beach is beside Anglesea River, the heath land around the area is diverse in its vegetation, and with over 80 orchid species it looks vibrant in springtime. Torquay is known as the surfing capital was previously named Spring Creek and is a rapidly expanding town. Point Danger provides great views out to sea; the reef just off Point Danger caused many a shipwreck, a large Anzac Memorial now sits on the headland.

Memorable Moments;

For anyone with a surfing interest visit; Surf World Museum in Torquay, learn about the culture surrounding surfing and the legends of the sport. (www.surfworld.com.au)

The major brands of surfing; Rip Curl and Quiksilver started life here, check out the shops that line Surf City Plaza on the Surfcoast Highway. Around the corner in Baines Court is a second's outlet.

Check out the Surf Coast walk that covers 44km of the coast line from Point Impossible north of Torquay to Fairhaven past Aireys Inlet. The walk is broken into 10 sections varying in difficulty, terrain and length. Point Addis Marine National Park is a protected haven for marine mammals and the nesting Hooded Plovers. Spend some time snorkelling at Point Danger reef, or swimming at Point Impossible or Southside beaches. Visit Coogoorah Park at the end of River Reserve Road, Anglesea, have a walk along the boardwalks through the wetlands.

Useful Information;

There is a good sized car park at the top of the cliff above Bells Beach providing an ideal vantage point to watch surfers. Compared with the big swells of Bells Beach, Jan Juc has wilder waves. During the summer months of December and January the surf coast becomes exceptionally busy, consider this in your planning. There is a large camping and caravanning area near Point Danger, across the road on Bell Street restaurants and a hotel. There is a large selection of accommodation catering particularly for those wanting to stay longer terms to enjoy the surf. Accommodation gets booked early, for those travelling the GOR in full length consider staying 22km away in Geelong or further down towards Cape Otway leaving the surf coast to the surf dudes. Information shelters car parks and restrooms are situated along the surf coast walk including; Anglesea, Point Addis, Bells Beach, Bird Rock Point Danger and Point Impossible. (www.surfcoast.vic.gov.au)

The Surf Coast

17 GEELONG

Situated 75km south of Melbourne, Geelong (pronounced Jillong) is the second most densely populated area in Victoria. Geelong sits on Corio Bay an inlet of Port Philip. On a clear day Melbourne skyline can be seen across the bay. During the 1800's settlers regularly travelled by steamer between Melbourne and Geelong. The area developed as the wool industry grew, and later during the gold rush experienced another population surge. Geelong became a large manufacturing area, for; wool, rope and paper. Since the 1920's fertiliser plants, the Ford Motor Company, Corio whisky distillery and the Shell oil refineries have joined the manufacturers in the area. The area has continued to expand with plans to develop further south of the city.

THE GREAT OCEAN ROAD

Memorable Moments;

The National Wool Museum provides an interesting history of the area and its wool trade since 1868 when Victoria opened its first woollen mill. Just a short walk up the road the town has some large shopping centres. Along the bay Cunningham Pier provides upmarket dining. The revamped waterfront is a nice walk, providing a range of gardens; children play areas and displays of local art works. Look out for the 100 "Bay walk Bollards" timber painted sculptures around the waterfront. Next to the pier is a modern glass building housing the steam driven Carousel. Boat trips can be taken out into Philip Bay. Have a walk around the town and enjoy some of the buildings of historical interest in the area.

Useful Information;

Geelong is the first major town before the start of the GOR when travelling from the east, making it an ideal stopping/starting place for a GOR trip. There is a huge choice of accommodation to suit all budgets, ample shops and hire cars can be picked up or dropped off in the area. The nearby Avalon airport is connected to Sydney by reasonable priced budget flights.

Melbourne is served by two airports; Tullamarine which is north of the city, and Avalon which is between Geelong and Melbourne. Tullamarine airport is 23km north from the city, and is better connected with domestic and international flights.

Avalon airport is 15km from Geelong along the Princes Freeway, or 55km south of Melbourne. Airport transport is available from Melbourne www.avalonairportshuttle.com.au flights from Avalon are limited to a domestic route to Sydney with Jetstar Airways. Budget, Avis and Europcar have desks inside Avalon airport and hire cars can be picked up and dropped off here.

M LEWIS

Mandy has written these books from her own experiences travelling, she combines her passion for travel with photography. She describes herself as a flash packer; a new era of traveler that is savvy, has electronic devices and wants to travel independently.

Look out for more in the flash packer series.

CPSIA information can be obtained
at www.ICGtesting.com
Printed in the USA
LVHW072116040419
613057LV00012B/350/P